NEWFOUNDLAND
JOURNEY ACROSS CANADA

Harry Beckett

The Rourke Book Co., Inc.
Vero Beach, Florida 32964

Harry Beckett M.A. (Cambridge), M.Ed. (Toronto), Dip.Ed. (Hull, England) has taught at the elementary and high school levels in England, Canada, France, and Germany. He has also travelled widely for a tour operator and a major book company.

Edited by Laura Edlund
Laura Edlund received her B.A. in English literature from the University of Toronto and studied Writing for Multimedia and Book Editing and Design at Centennial College. She has been an editor since 1986 and a traveller always.

ACKNOWLEDGMENTS
For photographs: Geovisuals (Kitchener, Ontario), The Canadian Tourism Commission and its photographers.
For reference: *The Canadian Encyclopedia, Encarta 1997, The Canadian Global Almanac, Symbols of Canada. Canadian Heritage*, Reproduced with the permission of the Minister of Public Works and Government Services Canada, 1997.
For maps: Promo-Grafx of Collingwood, Ont., Canada.

Library of Congress Cataloging-in-Publication Data

Beckett, Harry. 1936 -
   Newfoundland / by Harry Beckett.
     p. cm. — (Journey across Canada)
   Includes index.
   Summary: An introduction to the geography, history, economy, major cities, and interesting sites of Canada's easternmost province.
   ISBN 1-55916-197-3 (alk. paper)
   1. Newfoundland—Juvenile literature. [1. Newfoundland.]
I. Title II. Series: Beckett, Harry, 1936 - Journey across Canada.
F1122.4.B43 1997
971.8—dc21   97–2211
                                                    CIP
                                                     AC

Printed in the USA

TABLE OF CONTENTS

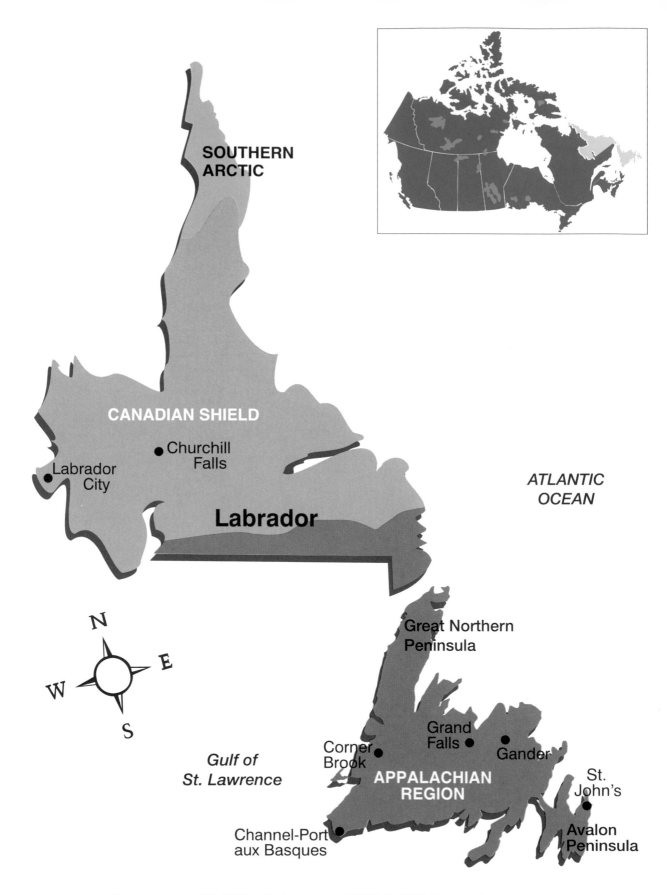

PROVINCE OF NEWFOUNDLAND

Chapter One
SIZE AND LOCATION

About a quarter of the province called Newfoundland is an island. This island can only be reached by ferry from the mainland or by air. It lies in the Atlantic Ocean across the mouth of the Gulf of St. Lawrence.

Labrador, north of the island and at the eastern end of mainland Canada, makes up the other three quarters.

The province extends a very long way from north to south. But what most people notice is how far east it is—Cape Spear is the most eastern part of North America. The island is closer to Ireland, across the Atlantic, than it is to Manitoba. Roads are few, and travel is often by ferry around the coast, where most of the settlements are.

Travel is even more difficult in Labrador than on the island. In winter, the land freezes and snowmobiles become important vehicles.

Find out more...

- The total area of the province is 405 720 square kilometres (15 660 square miles).
- Many settlements along the coast are called outports.

Chapter Two

GEOGRAPHY: LAND AND WATER

To most of us, Labrador would seem cold and wild. It is part of the **Canadian** (kuh NAY dee un) **Shield** (SHEELD), where much of the land is forest and rocks. Some of its people live on **fiords** (fyords), where the sea cuts into the land, but the bigger towns are inland.

Cape St. Mary's. Newfoundlanders call the island "the Rock."

Cape Race—the first land people see when coming to North America from Europe

On the island, mountains that are part of the Canadian Appalachians run up the western side into the Great Northern **Peninsula** (puh NIN soo la). People have settled wherever inlets provide shelter.

In the island's southeast corner is the Avalon Peninsula, with the capital city of St. John's and most other settlements.

Inland, the land is high, with wetlands and large forest areas.

Chapter Three

WHAT IS THE WEATHER LIKE?

The sea has a strong effect on Newfoundland's weather.

A warm ocean current comes up from the south, bringing air that is warm and moist. This warm air makes the climate milder around the Avalon Peninsula than on the rest of the island. But it also helps create fog, when the warm air meets cold air.

A cold current flows from the north down the east coast. Fish love these waters, and icebergs ride down on the cold current. They sometimes run aground and don't melt until late in the year.

The island's summers are cool and rainy; the winters are cold and snowy. Labrador has very cold and snowy winters. The summers there are also cool, but much less rainy than on the island.

An iceberg floats down the Newfoundland coast on the cold Labrador current.

F ind out more...

- The warm current is the Gulf Stream and the cold current is the Labrador Current.
- St. John's has average temperatures in July of 15.5°C (60° F) and in January, -3.9°C (24.8° F).

8

Chapter Four

MAKING A LIVING: HARVESTING THE LAND

With its **barren** (BARE en) soil and harsh climate, the island of Newfoundland lives up to its nickname—the Rock. Farming is very difficult. Most of it takes place on the island's Avalon Peninsula.

Logging provides wood for the important pulp and paper industry. Modern harvesting is very **mechanized** (MEK uh nized).

Newfoundlanders have always harvested the sea. Cod has been the traditional main catch. Boats from many nations fish in Newfoundland waters and the stocks have decreased. Lobster, squid, and scallops have become more important catches.

Harvesting logs for pulp and paper mills

Find out more...

- In Newfoundland, only 1/100 of the land is farmed.
- Halibut, haddock, and crab are also caught.

Chapter Five

FROM THE EARLIEST PEOPLES

Newfoundland's first peoples were called the **Beothuck** (BAY oe tuk). The last member of this nation died in 1829. Now, some **Micmac** (MIK mak) live on the south coast, **Inuit** (IN yoo it) on the northeast coast of Labrador, and **Montagnais-Naskapi** (mon tuh NYAY nus KA pee) in the interior.

A reconstructed Norse house at L'Anse aux Meadows

A fisherman and his grandson with their catch

Norse seafarers first landed here around A.D. 1000. Centuries later, English explorers claimed the land for their queen.

The first settlers, mostly English and Irish, built their homes in the sheltered sea coves near the fishing grounds. When the lumber industry and mining began, larger towns developed inland.

Newfoundland voted to join the Canadian Federation in 1949 and is the youngest province.

Chapter Six

Once fishing was the way most Newfoundlanders made a living. Now, many work in mining or in processing—turning raw fish, wood, and minerals into products. Wood, for example, can be made into newsprint or fence posts.

Other people work at the huge hydro-electric plant standing at Churchill Falls, or with the oil and gas found under the sea.

Most people, about 7 of every 10, work in the service sector—in government, transportation, and tourism, for example.

Find out more...

- Large amounts of iron are mined in Labrador
- Small amounts of other metals and minerals such as copper, nickel, zinc phosphorus, and asbestos are also mined.

The ferry is a main method of getting to "the Rock."

14

Chapter Seven

IF YOU GO THERE...

Would you like to watch whales? Boat trips to watch whales are very popular in Newfoundland. Visit Cape Spear and you may be lucky enough to see one leap from the sea!

During summer, tourists come to Signal Hill, above St. John's, to watch battles between the English and French armies re-enacted. Also on Signal Hill, Marconi received the first transatlantic radio message.

Gros Morne National Park offers wonderful scenery and outdoor activities for those who like hiking, boating, or swimming. Marble Mountain, near Corner Brook, is a great place to ski.

Old Cape Spear Lighthouse

Find out more...

- Marconi's message came from Cornwall, England, in 1901.
- Gros Morne is on the island's west coast.

Chapter Eight

MAJOR CITIES

St. John's, the capital, has been a safe harbour for 500 years. Surrounding hills and a long sea channel shelter it from the weather and the ocean. Rich fishing grounds are close by.

The houses are made of wood, and the city has been destroyed by fire several times.

Downtown St. John's, with colourful wooden houses and hilly streets

A typical outport with fishing boats

The Trans-Canada Highway links the city of St. John's to Gander, with its international airport, and to Corner Brook and the ferry port of Channel-Port aux Basques, on the west coast.

Labrador City is inland on the mainland, near the iron ore mines that give work to its people. It is close to the Québec border and ships its goods in and out by rail through that province.

Chapter Nine

SIGNS AND SYMBOLS

Newfoundland's flag contains many symbols. The white represents snow and ice. Blue stands for the sea. Red represents human effort, and the golden arrow is a sign of confidence and hope for the future. The red triangles stand for Labrador and the island. Look carefully to find a trident (three-pronged spear), which stands for fishing and the sea. When the banner hangs, the arrow becomes a sword to remind people of sacrifices in war.

The cross of Saint John the Baptist is on the coat of arms because the harbour of St. John's was discovered on his feast day. Lions and unicorns show the province's ties with Britain. Two Native figures represent the first peoples.

The motto is Latin and means "Seek ye first the Kingdom of God."

The provincial flower is the pitcher plant.

Newfoundland's flag, coat of arms, and flower

GLOSSARY

barren (BARE en) — not able to produce or grow things

Beothuk (BAY oe tuk) — an extinct Native people of Newfoundland

Canadian Shield (kuh NAY dee un SHEELD) — a horseshoe-shaped area of rock covering about half of Canada

fiord (fyord) — a long, steep-sided inlet from the sea

Inuit (IN yoo it) — Native people living in northern Canada and elsewhere

mechanized (MEK uh nized) — using machines

Micmac (MIK mak) — a Native people of eastern Canada

Montagnais-Naskapi (mon tuh NYAY nus KA pee) — a Native people of Québec, Labrador; the Innu

peninsula (puh NIN soo la) — a point of land almost surrounded by water

The re-enactment of a battle between the English and the French on Signal Hill

INDEX